A Walk With Summer

A Walk With Summer

15 Day Woman's Devotional

Summer Danielle

Xulon Press

Xulon Press
2301 Lucien Way #415
Maitland, FL 32751
407.339.4217
www.xulonpress.com

© 2022 by Summer Danielle

Michael Hoster -Photography
Gabriela Baca – Design Cover of Book
Xzavier Cox- Author Bio Photography

All rights reserved solely by the author. The author guarantees all contents are original and do not infringe upon the legal rights of any other person or work. No part of this book may be reproduced in any form without the permission of the author.

Due to the changing nature of the Internet, if there are any web addresses, links, or URLs included in this manuscript, these may have been altered and may no longer be accessible. The views and opinions shared in this book belong solely to the author and do not necessarily reflect those of the publisher. The publisher therefore disclaims responsibility for the views or opinions expressed within the work.

Unless otherwise indicated, Scripture quotations taken from the Holy Bible, New International Version (NIV). Copyright © 1973, 1978, 1984, 2011 by Biblica, Inc.™. Used by permission. All rights reserved.

Paperback ISBN-13: 978-1-66285-349-4
Ebook ISBN-13: 978-1-66285-350-0

Dedication

I dedicate this book to the one girl who just can't go any more. The girl who wants to give up. The one who has lost all hope, but also to the one that desires more in life, more of the Lord. The young woman who is tired of trying to fill this void deep within her- with everything, but God. This is for the woman who is ready, ready for more.

I would also like to acknowledge the Russell's. Without them what you are holding would not be a possibility. They were the Lord's hands and mouthpiece in orchestrating this book.

Let it be written, said, and fully known that the One and Only God, gets all the glory for this.

Table of Contents

Introduction: ix

Day 1: Surrender and Submission 1
Day 2: Tired and Tested 5
Day 3: When Storms Come ... Literally 11
Day 4: Horns of Hope 17
Day 5: When You're Not Okay 21
Day 6: Surrendered, So You Stay 25
Day 7: Immediate Obedience 31
Day 8: A Step of Faith 37
Day 9: Posture Of Waiting 43
Day 10: Humility 51
Day 11: Pregnant with a Promise 57
Day 12: Depressed and Distant 63
Day 13: Darkness of the Roots 67
Day 14: A Test of Your Heart 73
Day 15: Wait And Praise 77
Day 16: Final Recap 83

Closing: 85
Connect with Author: 87

Introduction

Hello, my friend. My name is Summer, and what you have in your hands is a collection of events in my life that shows when my life truly began. I began this book with a bit of a backstory of what my life looked like before accepting the Lord into my heart, while also building momentum to how exactly I got here. He began instructing me to start writing almost immediately after I accepted Him into my heart, but I did not start writing until the months to follow when I could no longer fight off the clear command from heaven. Writing, I thought, was not a strong suit of mine, so I assumed either He was crazy for instructing me to write or I was crazy for hearing voices! The truth is writing is one of my weaknesses. But does anyone know what the Lord does with human weaknesses? "But he said to me, 'My grace is sufficient for you, for my power is made perfect in weakness.' Therefore, I will boast more gladly about my weaknesses, so that Christ's power may rest on me" (2 Cor. 12:9). That is exactly why and how you are holding these pages in your hands right now. You are holding the faithfulness of God in what He does with our weaknesses. You are holding the results of pure obedience and faith. This right here should be a big enough sign and spark of faith to step out and do as He has commanded you, especially if it involves a weakness of yours.

This book has been sifted and combed through to grab only the sections that would hopefully bless your life, encourage your heart, and inspire you to step out in faith and obedience, like I have. I hope I can accomplish that, if you'll just give me fifteen days. I believe the Lord has anointed me for such a time as this to be a part of this season in your life—to walk with you together and share stories and events from my life with you, showing how God showed up and how I, a child of God, worked through these situations as well. Some of the things I write about are tough and may surprise you to read, but my heart is that you don't focus on the story but on the Lord's hand *inside* the story. Ask the Lord along the way to reveal to your heart how this applies to you and your relationship with Him. Find the ways you can grow as a believer in your relationship with God. So, my friend, may we begin this journey together? Open your eyes to see the Lord and open your heart to be changed by Him. Let us pray before we embark upon this journey of growth together.

Introduction

Dear Heavenly Father,

Praise you, my God. You are good, and Your mercy endures forever. Thank you, Lord, for Your faithfulness and for Your loving kindness that is sweet, pure, and never changes. Please open my eyes to see You in my life, Lord, and how You are moving and have a purpose for me. Please soften and quiet my heart today as I seek You and may my heart be receptive to receive all that You are trying to do in me. Purify, refine, and mold me together. I am Yours and Yours completely. Come and have your way in me today and every single day. As I read this book, I ask that I would not be the same by the end of it. Continue working in me and speak to me clearly through the words I read.

In Jesus's name, Amen.

Now, something you will notice to be a bit different about this group of papers in your hand is the way I decided to end each section, with a prayer and application with some questions to really push growth in your heart. It is so important to me that we grow and learn but also that we apply what we learn and allow it to stick to us and change us from the inside out. The book of James talks about the importance of applying what you learn in listening and doing. Chapter 1 verse 22 says,

"Do not merely listen to the word, and so deceive yourselves. Do what it says." Verse 25 continues, "...not forgetting what they have heard, but doing it—they will be blessed in what they do." We know this is something very important to James but also to the Lord. There is a process all believers will go through that forms and molds their heart along with their character. For that to happen, we must be actively applying the wisdom we acquire that can be found in and from the Lord. "For the Lord gives wisdom; from his mouth comes knowledge and understanding" (Prov. 2:6 NIV).

So, at the end of each section, I have added questions, applicable suggestions, and different scriptures to also back up why I have even chosen to write on the topic. I desire for you to know that what you are reading is not what is in my heart for you but from your Father's heart. He had a plan for you to hold this collection of events and stories of some young woman like myself with the intention of your heart being sparked with courage to run to your Father. Hit your knees before Him and wait for Him to speak. Use this to open the door to listen, then let me lead you to apply what you learn and gather from the Holy Spirit. Let's do it together. Let's commit to this, my friend, and see what God does. Does that sound good?

I would like to talk about myself before we begin so you guys get to know me a little better to bring validity to the things I will be sharing. I did not have the easiest childhood in the world, but then again, does anyone really? I know there are many things for me to be thankful for and trust me, I am, but I am also not going to gloss over the traumatic things I went through. I am going to bring to light the difficulties and heartaches I experienced so I can speak about the faithfulness and love of Jesus Christ, bringing all the glory to His name. It is for certain that I have had a very trauma-filled life starting at a young age. But the Lord is good, amen? I have witnessed the faithfulness of God in how He would work everything for my good. Romans 8:28 says, "And we know that in all things God works for the good of those who love him, who have been called according to his purpose." Without the traumas of my life, I would not be who I am today. I would most likely not even know the Lord and would not be completely in love and steadfast for Him. I have had so many opportunities to encourage and inspire someone to run with God with everything in them because of what I've been through. Because of this, I would do it over again. Temporary pain for eternal glory.

Back to my childhood, it was tough growing up. My family was broken and experienced many hardships. I struggled as an individual in several ways at way too young of an age and on way too many occasions. It really began when I was born into a broken marriage. From the start, my parents did not build themselves on the only foundation that is sustainable in this damaged world we live in. They attempted to build a family on this shaky and unstable ground, which is where I come in. I was the icing on the cake. My birth shook their ground up more, resulting in tumultuous events. My dad started drinking a lot, and then fifteen months later, my sister was born—another baby born into what was already a broken and godless home. This caused our family to come crashing down. My parents fought and fought so much that it began to get physical. This wasn't something my mother wanted her two little ones to be around, so she made the only decision she knew to make but was still one of the hardest choices she would ever make—to leave my dad. There was a bit of back and forth, I vaguely remember, until my mom decided she was going to leave North Carolina and go back home to Ohio with us. My mom and sister left North Carolina, but I decided that I wanted to stay with my dad, and so I did. I was just five years old at the time. Big, big mistake. My dad, being completely distraught by the situation, he turned to even heavier drinking and partying, running to women for comfort. (My dad ended up marrying one of the women later in their lives and having my little sister.) All the while his five-year-old daughter was in the other room. I remember parties with so many people and smoke filling the house. My dad would lock himself in his room for hours, and I would lay on my back in front of the door, just kicking and kicking on it. I would be begging and crying for my dad to come out, but he wouldn't. He made it very clear that I was obviously not a priority in his life. This quickly became a truth planted in the pit of the person I was becoming. Praise God, I was very mature at my age, and I was able to sustain myself by myself. I would make food for myself and make plans to go over to my neighbor's house to not be alone. I would even find my own ways to school—*that is called the favor of God.*

Now, at the time, I had no idea what was going on, but this didn't stop the situation from ultimately warping my heart and planting so many deep-rooted things that would affect me all the way into adulthood. There came a point where my mom could no longer get a hold of me, so she finally reached out to my nearby family. One day, I was laying on the couch with my dad and some woman when my uncle came in and asked if I wanted to go to our cousin's house. He wasn't just taking me to my cousin's house, though; he was taking me away from my dad. My family had plotted a plan to get me to my mom for my protection. But this resulted in many of my dad's family relationships ending. My uncles got together and decided what they knew would cost them my dad but was needed. They drove me to my grandpa's house, and at five years old, I flew on a plane to Ohio, alone. When my mom got me off the plane, she immediately had doctor's appointments lined up to make sure I was okay. I wasn't. Besides having psychological issues, I was surprisingly still high on the drugs that had been coursing through the house for days and days. My mom did her best to help me get into therapy to try and talk through all that had happened in hopes of mending her broken little girl, but the damage was already done. Now the healing that I was in desperate need of was only going to come from One source. It just took me some years to find it. In the years following, the battles and traumas did not stop hitting me from every side:

- My mom's abusive boyfriend who we lived with for too long.
- The many times I was taken advantage of physically.
- Being homeless, on multiple occasions.
- Move after move after move we made.

Some of the biggest things that I needed as a child were consistency, community, and love but I never had them … until God.

Right before I decided to pick up my life and move four hours away from my alma mater town to Wilmington, North Carolina, my life changed. Forever. It did a complete 180-degree flip and took us all by surprise. You see, the five years I had lived in this previous town, I had really made a name for myself. I did have quite a bit of friends, you could say, and was known for being big into partying. I was super social and liked to have a good time, party, drink, and smoke weed. So, when I say the life change took us all by surprise, it really did.

Before this time in my life, I would always say had a relationship with God, and it was an okay one. I always talked to Him, prayed when I needed to, and went to church as often as possible. What was holding me back, however, was that I never really took the next step in cutting out ungodly and impure things in my life. I wasn't yielding and living my life with God and wasn't living it for Him. But, as I slowly started to approach this season in my life, I noticed Him drawing me closer. I started to hear Him calling my name and pulling me in. I still wasn't ready, though. I was fixed on numbing the pain of life by getting high and drunk, and I wasn't ready to give that up. Until July the 16th, 2018, the most critical turning point in my life. Leading up to this day, I was slowly but aggressively being chipped away at until I was no more. My life up to this moment had been tough. I struggled. I was hurting and broken and didn't even know it. On this specific day, I was done trying with life. I was too tired to pick up all my broken pieces scattered across the floor and was ready to go, ready to give up. Are you curious about what got me here exactly? It was the death of my one-month-old brother passing away before I even had the chance to meet him. He was the product of a five-year-long affair of my dad on my stepmom. I was already completely broken and beat down from my childhood and so depressed, so this just pushed me over the ledge that I was already struggling to balance on. So, like I said, I was done. But, I thought, *Maybe I will give this "Jesus" thing one more shot.* He had been softening my heart ever so slightly in the months prior to this moment, so when I got to the end, I knew this was the only other place to go. He was drawing me so close to Him even though I was busy living to satisfy my flesh. I would literally get done with drinking and hanging out with boys at 4:00 am and still leave at 7:00 am to drive an hour and half to church the next morning. He was drawing me out, and He did not care what I was doing. He just wanted me and all of me, not just on Sundays. So, I decided to give it one more shot and try reading my Bible and see if anything would happen. Attempting to read my Bible, I started like any severely-depressed nineteen-year-old would; I looked up scriptures for depression and came across Deuteronomy 31:8. I flipped open my Bible to begin looking for this verse in a book that I knew next to nothing about, especially where anything was, and opened it not just to Deuteronomy but specifically Deuteronomy 31:8, with the page folded down covering verse 8 in the top right of the page: "The Lord himself goes before you and will be with you; he will never leave you nor forsake you. Do not be afraid; do not be discouraged." As I read the words that were now uncovered to me, the truth of it was also uncovered to me in my heart. The Lord let me know in that moment that He saw me. *He saw me* and has been with me every single moment of my life. He spoke so clearly that day in my bedroom to a hopeless, broken, little girl. That's all I needed to know. I laid my life down and was completely committed and devoted to living the rest of my life with Him in mind. That day, I made up my mind that my life was His now.

Most of my friends expected that I would soon go back to my old lifestyle, but one friend, my future roommate, joined me in our commitment to Christ. During the summer of 2018 and being the life of the party and having so much fun hanging out with not the best people, a good friend and I decided that we wanted to make a change. We decided that we wanted to take this whole "Jesus" thing to the next level. For us, we knew that meant we needed to make some lifestyle changes, and we were ready. No more drinking or partying. No more hanging out with our huge friend group either, so we bounced out of the blue. These were huge decisions and commitments to two nineteen-year-old girls. We decided that we were swapping all that out for daily devoted time with God. Our first day doing this, we decided to meet at a local coffee shop to read and study the Bible together. We got there, ordered our drinks, sat on the couch in the back of the room in front of the window, got all our things out, and we heard, "Oh my gosh!" I looked up and could not even believe who was in front of me, and I can still remember the face she made. It was my old friend. We had lost contact over silly high school reasons, but here she was, right in front of me. Her expression made a lot more sense after she reached in her bag to grab her Bible. She had really come to the same place as us, at the same time as us, to do the same exact thing. My friend had decided that she was was also in a place where she wanted to make some lifestyle changes that included being more devoted to the Lord. Now she was not in the same place my other friend and I had been in, like partying and drinking every weekend, but she more or so was distracted by boys and things of life. We all made it together at this cute coffee shop, a divine orchestration of the Lord that would impact all of us, forever.

    As soon as I started to cut out all the community that had no intentions in pushing me forward in my relationship with the Lord, He blessed me with a community that would do just that.

A couple of my friends, and I began this journey meeting as many times a week as possible at this coffee shop to do our daily devotional and talk about the Lord. Of course, this required us to spend way too much money on coffee and overpriced (yet oh so delicious) Caesar salads. I received a little gift card from one of the employees because I was a "loyal customer"— aka, "You spend too much money here, and we are sorry; here is a token of our apologies!" These were the times I looked forward to the most, the moments that got me through the rough times at home. They kept me steadfast when I stressed and worried about things of the future, like how I was possibly going to afford Wilmington by myself.

Like I mentioned, we started to cut out activities and lifestyle things like smoking weed, drinking, and partying. We cut out cursing and talking to boys. Anything that was not a good influence on us or our relationship with the Lord was out. We even deleted our social media apps. We girls were not playing around, but sadly, this came at a price. Making these unpopular decisions, we became infamous in our small little town. The sad thing about the negative attention that we were getting is that it was coming from my "friends." It hurt and really had me rethinking what we were doing a little, honestly. No matter what was said or what happened, however, we were not backing down—well, *I* wasn't. Even though we had these bumps in the road and the devil coming for our throats, we held each other together with love and encouragement. We were accountable for the things we saw in each other that were holding us back from charging toward Jesus more and gave each other advice to get past these bumps. We were getting closer and closer to God, and for the first time in my life, I felt like I had joy. I could feel sparks of joy igniting in my heart and soul. It was amazing! I was not going to be shaken off the 80-mph train faced directly at the throne of God.

I mentioned before that I was getting ready to move to Wilmington. This happened to be the first attempt of the enemy to get me off this train. Moving to Wilmington was hard. It was not something a nineteen-year-old should have been doing on her own, I know that much. I was without a job and trying to buy everything I needed with funds that were quickly running out. *That* was the least of things. A few weeks passed, groceries were needed, and bills were beginning to add up. Before I knew it, I was completely out of money. I had to go without things nobody should. I had no family to help me move in, so there was surely no family to fall back on in times of financial instability. In this journey and season of lack that I was in, I quickly recognized that my Father is a faithful God. He is Jehovah Jireh, my provider. I am His child, so He will provide for me. My job is to have faith—to trust and keep my focus on Him, being obedient to His Word and commands. He is my Father, and He will make a way, even when there seems to be absolutely no way. In a season of lack, these are our job duties. We are to not worry or wonder what we will possibly do but look to our Father who art thou in heaven enthroned above us. He is our God and provider. I never had consistency from someone who provided for me in life, so this was a nugget of wisdom that would take time for me to grasp completely. A provider was not a part of my vocabulary and Someone who I didn't even know and could not even see doing it—it was a stretch, but in this season, knowing that God was now my provider was a foundation that He was building. It was DIFFICULT. I struggled, but the Lord was so patient in showing His loving kindness until I finally caught on. He was understanding of the difficulty I was having and was right there to prove to me time and time again that He was trustworthy, stable, consistent, and loving, and that He indeed was going to provide for me in all areas of my life.

Enough about my move, for now. I am going to start breaking down specific events and lessons that I learned in Wilmington.

I know that was a lot, so why don't we begin our fifteen days tomorrow?

Today, I just ask that you go to the Lord your Father and ask Him to prepare your heart for the next fifteen days—for what He intends for you to experience, how He wants you to grow and what He wants you to better understand. Let us prepare our hearts to hear from the King of kings.

DAY 1
Surrender and Submission

Two words I believe that we must completely and fully grasp before truly stepping into a successful relationship with the King of kings. We must first fully surrender our life to Him. We must deny our flesh and completely. Once we complete this, then we can move on to the submission of our God and His ways. Submission without surrender can become a bit messy and can turn into inconsistency. It becomes a thing we practice only when it is convenient for us—when we desire to submit to, and only then. I don't believe this submission pleases our God. Submission is the action of yielding to someone superior. What does this mean for a follower of Jesus? It means we set our desires below Gods desires for us and align our life with this. This is wisdom I was blessed with, almost immediately, in my walk with the Lord at nineteen years old. I knew from the very beginning that due to the fire burning in me for a relationship with the Lord, I could not partake in almost anything I had prior to knowing Him. I could not have the same friends. I could not do the same things or be at the same places. So, what did I do? I yielded myself to God. I submitted to Him and His authority, and although He never once told me to stop any of it, I was under His authority, so He never had to. I had placed myself under His authority; therefore, I desired nothing other than to be submitted to His plans for my life. Let's look at what the Word says about submission and surrendering to the Lord. I think Luke 22:42 paints a picture of the most beautiful image of what submission to the Lord and surrendering your desires to His really looks like. In this passage, we see Jesus immediately following the Last Supper with all His disciples. He then goes to the Mount of Olives to pray and cry out to His Father. You know what is coming next, and so did Jesus. He was struggling with what He knew was coming soon. He hit His knees before the Lord and cried out an earth-shattering prayer that should be on a mantle every believer strives to get to one day. "Father, if you are willing, take this cup from me; yet not my will, but yours be done." (Luke 22:42) This is absolutely mind-boggling to me because it is not the way our human minds desire to think, feel, or speak in times of suffering and hardship. Our innate reaction and response are quite opposite. It is to retreat and run away in fear, but this is exactly what true submission and surrender looks like. You do not think of yourself and your own plans, and if you do, at the end of the day, you still throw them away to pick up your Father's instead.

Application:

What area of your life have you not quite surrendered to the Lord completely?

Has the Lord spoken to you already about an area of your life that you have not surrendered to Him?

What do you think is necessary for you to do to get to this place of surrender that Jesus walked in daily?

Seek the Lord; seek Him now. Ask Him to help you step deeper into your submission to Him and His plans for your life. I promise they are much better than yours and more than you could ever ask, think, or imagine for yourself.

> Ephesians 3:20—"Now to him who is able to do immeasurably more than all we ask or imagine, according to his power that is at work within us."
>
> Jeremiah 29:11—"He has a plan and a purpose for your life. Plans to prosper you, not to harm you but to give you a hope and a future."

Trust Him, my friend, and surrender your life and plans for His and see what happens. He is a good God, and He does good things.

DAY 2

Tired and Tested

So, yesterday was one of the hardest days of my life. I had a panic attack. If you haven't had one before, you are very fortunate, and I hope you go your entire life without one. To describe to you what mine are like, it starts off by crying that turns into hyperventilating that slowly and painfully turns into numbness and tingling in my hands and face. My hands cramp up and freeze almost, along with my mouth. This panic attack, I couldn't move or breathe and could barely even talk. Between my aggressive short inhales and hardly having the strength to open my mouth, I managed to call my best friend. I somehow was able to mumble enough words out to explain my situation to her and that I needed help. In what seemed like hours, she was finally able to calm me down enough so I could drive home. It was only a few minutes down the road until my thoughts began to race and replay all that had happened, and I started hysterically crying all over again. Tears filling my eyes, I was struggling to see the road. When I finally got home and could call my best friend and explain what had caused this terrible incident, it happened again. Within minutes, I began to cry and struggled to get words out. I was just holding onto hearing her words of encouragement and peace. She then began telling me exactly what I needed to hear but not even close to what I wanted to hear. It didn't consist of anything I was expecting to hear or desiring to hear in a time of pain. She was encouraging me, yes, but to keep going. To run to God, and He would provide strength. Even though I was responding negatively, saying I couldn't do what she was asking me to do, I knew I needed to. She didn't back down but kept repeating it, and it was eating me alive. We changed the subject and got in a few giggles and stories before my roommate got home and I quickly recapped the terrible event, but my roomate had a completely different response and perspective to the situation. You see, God blessed me with two close friends in this season with two different types of friendship. My roommate was telling me what I was thinking and exactly what my flesh was searching for. Not until later did I realize that this was a test, and my flesh was not the way I was going to get through this. I began to go on about how I didn't understand why this was happening. I was struggling so much at this time in what seemed to be every area of my life, so I just couldn't understand why my job had to be one of those areas. I was just trying to work to pay my bills and be a light there, loving my coworkers. My focus was to spend time with the Lord, but needing to pay my bills, I also needed to work. Let me break down this season in my life a bit more. Maybe you've been here before. Maybe you're here now, so may this encourage you.

This season in my life, "adulting" was new, and paying for many bills, alone, was difficult. To afford my cost of living, I was working two jobs, and not much money was left over each month. I was waiting tables six or seven days a week and working at a smoothie café making food and smoothies five or six days a week. I was working anywhere from sixty-two hours a week to one week around the holidays, I remember working closer to eighty hours. I worked seven days a week, and most of those days consisted of working both jobs—one with a 7:00 am clock in, and the other with a 10:30 pm clock out. I don't need to explain the obvious symptoms from this type of lifestyle...I was tired. I was exhausted. I was so beyond overworked that I was having at least one mental breakdown a week. Anything and everything pushed me completely off a cliff and took time for me to recover, climbing back up the side of the rocky ledge. But I did. Every single time, for the Lord. I vividly remember days of feeling so helpless, hopeless, and alone. Life just seemed to be too much for me at times. I was battling with suicidal thoughts and would often cry myself to sleep, not wanting to wake up. I wanted to give up time and time again. But God; His mercies were always new and were always waiting on me in the morning. Lamentation 3:22 says, "The steadfast love of the Lord never ceases; his mercies never come to an end; they are new every morning; great is your faithfulness." Great is His faithfulness, and every single time. The Lord was there for me every single morning, waiting for me with His peace and love. I was back on what I was there for, to live for God. I remember I would cry out to Him asking for forgiveness for wanting to give up, basking in His love and faithfulness knowing that everything was okay because I was in His will. Praise God.

So, any who, why the panic attack? Super small incident, in my opinion, but a test I can see it as now. A bit of fire applied to my season to test my character and faithfulness to the Lord. A test in the middle of my tiredness. (I'll unpack this faithfulness a bit later.) Ending my shift at the smoothie cafe, I decided to order my lunch, which was free after each shift. My co-worker asked a simple, completely harmless question, if I ever had that smoothie with peanut butter before, and if I wanted to try it. Our manager overheard our conversation and began yelling at me for not paying for the .99 cent scoop of peanut butter my co-worker offered to toss in my smoothie. We started telling our manager that we weren't trying to steal and did not think it was a big deal and I could pay for it, no problem. Well, she did not have any desire to hear us out and continued yelling over me, not even letting me speak. I remembered feeling like a pet dog with the way she was speaking over me. She rang up my scoop of peanut butter for $1.07. I was so hurt that I had been screamed at and just completely disrespected, but I went out to my car to get my wallet. I looked inside, and I only had two, one-dollar bills. As I grabbed my last two dollars, I completely lost it. I ran back inside to give my coworker the money and trying to choke back my tears in my throat, I gasped for air and told her to just keep it. I went back to my car, the scene of this panic attack.

Application:

Have you been here before?

Maybe there wasn't a peanut butter scoop involved, but what I mean is, have you ever been here, walking on the ledge of a mountain? Uneven ground. Rocks crumbling below your feet with every step. Unsteady ground, causing even your emotions to be unsteady. Tired. In my case, physically, but maybe in your case, emotionally or mentally tired. Then amidst your paralyzing weariness, you're tested. Then what?

When you are in a season of struggle and hardship and life cannot seem to stir anymore, then heat is applied. What should we do?

What is God desiring us to do when we are tried by fire?

Will you stay at a job God clearly confirmed, but you are undervalued, underpaid, and disrespected there?

Will you be a faithful, hard worker?

Will you respect your boss who continues to disrespect you?

How will you react when you're tired and tested?

DAY 3

When Storms Come... Literally

You see, the thing with storms are, they tend to come at the worst possible moments in our lives. They often show up during an already disrupted season of life. A week or two later after this terrible incident, the last thing I needed to happen, happened. I finally was getting in the hang of this thing called life. I was working two jobs and about to start making money and getting my life together, financially. I mean, life was really looking up. All that talk about "My life is going to get better" and "God will provide and take care of me" was really happening. Things were still difficult, but hey, I saw progression and was running with it as fast as I could and hopefully into the next season. Then, just like that, a hurricane came to not only destroy Wilmington but also all the progress that I had made. It was going to directly hit Wilmington, so we had to evacuate because it was going to be a category 5 and wipe out the east coast. Let me say that again just in case you missed it- a few days after my life was really looking up, when I really started becoming a stress-free gal, a category 5 hurricane was coming and I had to evacuate and leave this place that I had finally come to, to be washed away with the waves. This meant so many things. No job. No income. Again. This meant going back to my alma mater town and living in a far from godly household, a town filled with past mistakes and possible current temptations. Leaving my new home filled with all my things to be possibly destroyed. But I was not just leaving physical things in my apartment; I was leaving my hope behind too. This hope I had worked so incredibly hard to just barely wrap my fingers around to pick it up and place it in my heart, and what now? Just up and snatched out of my hands. I so quickly fell back into that place of darkness and depression. With all these feelings completely drowning me and confusion surrounding me, I was also in a house full of anger and sin. I was physically digging myself into a deeper hole, letting the enemy be the loudest voice in my head and make my decisions for me. I was falling deep and fast into this hole of despair and desperation for change.

    You see, the thing about this hole is that I was the only reason and cause for being in it. "I" was listening to the enemy say, "Jump in." "I" was listening to the enemy to make my decisions. This was on me this time. I so effortlessly began digging the hole with my thoughts, then looked to the enemy, and with confidence, jumped inside. This hole I am referring to is a distraction and an attempt from your enemy to get you off the path that gets you to your purpose and calling. It's a Distance from the path. You can spot it from afar, but until you start thinking thoughts you should not and listening to the one who wants you gone, it's already beneath your feet. Your eyes come off your God and the path He has for you and onto yourself, your circumstance, and your enemy; and now you're in the hole. I think of the story of when Peter walked on water. He so confidently jumped out of the boat in faith on just one word. He walked to his Father, and before his Father's face, he felt a gust of wind and was afraid. He took his face off his Father who was right in front of him and placed his eyes on the wind he could not even see. Peter then immediately sank. I believe we as believers sometimes do this very thing. We see the winds of life, the storms required in a specific season, and look away from the Lord. We become afraid, and we sink into the closest hole to us. The storms are not meant to take us out; they're meant to elevate us in our character and relationship with the Lord, but we often miss this—well, I do.

    It wasn't anyone's fault but mine that I was in the place I was in this time. Yes, my circumstances were a bit tough, we can all agree, but in a season that I should have run to Jesus, I ran to the nearest hole. I was only thinking about all that was not going right in my life, seeking God but mainly to ask, "Why are You allowing this to happen to me?" Instead, I should have taken a small step back for just a moment to look at my life and not just my current circumstances. I should have looked to my God with questions with His glory in mind.

Questions like, "How can I grow in this? How can I give You the most glory in this? What are You looking for from me, in this?" Thinking thoughts, wondering what the Lord may have in mind to use this for my good. "Maybe this place of darkness is actually where God is molding me. Maybe in this place of lack, the Lord is growing my dependency and trust in Him. Maybe what feels like a fiery furnace is just the place where the Lord is burning things off me, chains and traumas. Maybe, just maybe, this specific time in my life is for my good and the Lord's glory." For all of this to be true, I needed to completely surrender this situation, to get out of this hole and lay the season at God's feet, to cry out to Him not to change it but to change my heart. A willing and surrendered heart is key for a refined and transformed heart, so that's exactly what I decided to do.

Application:

Are you currently in one of these holes? Sharing a seat with the enemy?

What is one actionable step you can begin right *now* to actively crawl out? To encourage yourself to take hold of the rocky side of the hole you fell into and pull yourself up?

Maybe you're not in one now, but let's be prepared so when one is presented, we can avoid it completely.

Write out three steps for your *survival guide* if you do find yourself looking at a hole directly in front of you. Now, write out three things to work into your daily routine to keep you from even looking away from the Lord for one second and jumping into one.

Examples could be memorizing or quoting scriptures every morning or planning intentional quiet time with the Lord when you spend time in your Bible and talking to God before you even begin your day.

What does it look like to protect yourself from falling into a hole of weariness, doubt, or fear?

_____

_____

_____

_____

_____

_____

_____

_____

A Walk With Summer - 15 Day Devotional

DAY 4

Horns of Hope

This will be a quick one, meant to be just a reminder and a spark of encouragement for the one who is in a season of frustration, confusion, and doubt, wondering what exactly the Lord is doing. If the things He has shown you in dreams and whispered to your heart long ago have seemed to die in this season. Let me speak something to you quickly. Open your heart to truly receive it so you can keep going. Keep seeking His face and eventually watch these things unfold.

Losing faith and hope are two things that begin to occur when things get a little rough. When life gets tough, these are the first things we want to throw out of our lives when they are crucial to getting to the next season. The unfair thing is these are also the two things that we should be clinging to in hopes they increase when we are in the storms of life. This is how we please the Lord, having faith for the things that are not yet visible to us, faith to look with the eyes of the Holy Spirit who is all knowing, not from our flesh eyes that are easily deceived.

My friend, hear me out. This is critical for what happens next in your life. Have faith. Grab enough hope deep down. Find the words He once spoke, and which seemed so clear at one time in your life. Scoop up the hope hovering over them, and grab ahold of it, having faith that you do indeed, serve a faithful King. Have such a faith that what He spoke, will come; that what He showed you, you will walk into; that He is a good God and a faithful Father. Things are changing in what seems to be an unchanging season. There may not be outward visible changes but let me assure you that there are so many inward changes that you are undergoing. Have faith that He has a plan and purpose for your life, and guess what? It is to give you a hope and future, to prosper you, and not to harm you! And that is a promise! So, let's grab hope by the horns and not let go. I know it is hard, but go through the Lord, and He will give you the strength to do it!

Application:

If your heart has ever been in a place of hopelessness or maybe it is now, could I encourage you? Encourage you to press in. Keep going even if you feel like you cannot. Cry out to your Father and ask for His peace that surpasses all understanding and peace that pleases your heart so much, so you begin running. Turn your eyes from all those emotions and look up my friend. To your Father. To the King of the world. To The Creator of all and everything. He has you, I promise.

Can I also encourage you that if it seems like you are fighting battle after battle-there is a reason! There are hands to be equipped to hold what the Lord has for you. There is a heart to be chastened to look more like Christ's. There is character to be molded for the promises the Lord has anointed you to walk into. Praise Him through the storms because we know exactly who He is and How He operates. How much He loves and cares for us. There is something significant about praising the Lord during battles. In the midnight hour like Paul and Silas in prison, when the shackles fell and broke. There is breakthrough. Keep going.

Press in and praise Him until it happens.

What does it look like to praise your heavenly Father today?

Remind yourself of ways that the Lord has shown up in your life in the past.

Read Psalm 34 and see David's heart posture during a storm. Write out three verses that you are going to apply to your heart in this storm, or the next.

Write out three praises to the Lord.

A Walk With Summer - 15 Day Devotional

DAY 5
When You're Not Okay

Honestly, at this very moment in my life, I am not okay. This point in the journey, this place in the process, it is safe to say that I am not okay. This balancing game that I have been playing on the ledge of life for so long, it is exhausting. I have exerted so much energy and so much strength for so long, I think I have run out. I have now fallen off the mountain side, and it feels like there is no saving me. I feel as though I am at a point in my life where I cannot take anything else. I am no longer in the place of just trying to survive, I am physically trying to climb up the backside of this mountain I have just tumbled down. I am just trying to save my own life from life itself, every single day and moment.

So, like I said, I am not okay, but I think that's okay. I think it is okay that I do not feel like I am okay right now. I don't think that is an expectation the Lord has for us when we are going through the trials of life to build and grow us. I think it is just fine that we are not always fine. Now, what you do in the times of feeling completely beat down and even falling down the side of the mountain you were in the process of climbing, I believe is very important! There are expectations the Lord has on us in how we respond to us not being okay. Your heart posture toward Him, has it shifted? Your perspective on life, has that changed at all? There are things that I believe the Lord is focused on in this time to see what exactly you do and where you go. Is your heart still postured toward Him? Is your perspective pointed up to the top of the mountain and not to give up?

Application:

My friend, evaluate your heart and your life if you feel as though now, or at one time in your life, you did not feel like you were okay or could go any further. You could not navigate one more situation. You were not able to make it through another trial or gust of wind to throw you off the side of the mountain you have been fighting to make up.

Ask the Lord to search your heart and reveal to you any areas that are not honoring Him, any areas of your life that are not aligning with the expectation that He has for this season. Read Psalm 149 and see David's heart when he was seeking God to reveal areas of his own heart that were not honoring to Him.

In James 1, verse 1 we are commanded to consider our rough seasons filled with tribulation as pure joy, he calls it. To consider this, we must be so intentional about how we view our season of struggle. We must have God switch our perspective and must be intentional about considering it completely joyful because we know our God's character.

If we keep reading in James 1, he explains that we should have these thoughts because from these trials, it tests our faith and creates perseverance in us. The genuineness of our faith will be proven in these refining and sifting seasons, and this is crucial if the Lord is going to use us to help build His kingdom. Perseverance, to be patiently faithful without complaining or getting angry, is something that is also a necessity for the servants of God to build His kingdom.

So, as a recap, let us count it as pure joy when we are not okay because we are being refined by God with the hopes that our character will be refined to the Lord's likeness.

We may not be okay, but oh will we be in the end!

_____

_____

_____

_____

A Walk With Summer - 15 Day Devotional

DAY 6
Surrendered, So You Stay

I have never worked so much in my entire time. I calculated it, and after tomorrow's shift, I will be right up to seventy hours. Seventy hours of physical laboring on my feet and talking to people is emotionally draining. At one of the two jobs I currently work, I make quite a bit of money. The other job is probably the lowest paying job in all of Wilmington. Not putting much thought into it, I decided I would quit the lower paying job and just work the higher paying one. So, at a movie the other day with my friend, I quickly typed up my resignation letter on Gmail and sent it to my boss. I clicked send, set the phone down, and looked up to see the Lord fold His arms, sit back, and say to me, "Summer, you did not talk to Me about this." Sounds crazy, but I am telling the truth! This is the way it went down. Being a new believer, I am still navigating the whole "submitting to the Lord's will in my life" thing. The submission part has never been the problem; it is how you execute it in day-to-day life situations that has been a little difficult. I was not sure how exactly to respond to the God of the universe getting a bit of 'tude with me and without hesitation questioning my actions. So, after I finished the movie, I went home and sought the Lord. I began pouring out the truest part of my heart to Him, which was to please Him and be in His will. I repented to Him and expressed how sorry I was and that if He gave me another chance, I would make it right. I asked for wisdom and guidance, and I received it. I told Him if He wanted me to stay, I would, but I needed an opportunity to do so.

I came into work the following Monday, and the owner came in right behind me and walked up to me to explain how sad he was that I was leaving. He asked me a very simple question that left my heart completely shaken. He asked me if I would stay if he promoted me and gave me a raise. Wow! Forget the difficulty that comes with working two jobs or even fifty-two jobs, the Lord just proved His faithfulness and commitment to me in those very simple questions. This encounter brought my kneel of surrender before the throne of God a bit deeper. If the Lord was going to be faithful to a simple request of giving me another opportunity, I was surely going to be faithful to stay at a job that paid next to nothing and was running me into the ground. This time around, I was going to stay however long the Lord kept me there. I was already struggling working two jobs, but this was a clear sign that the Lord wanted me at this job and for whatever reason. That reason was not for me to know; all I needed to do was stay, and so I did. I stayed because I surrendered my emotions and surrendered to His will for my life.

Fast forward six months, and I find out exactly why the Lord had me stay. You see, the Lord has already gone forward and back in my life and yours. He has days ordained and times appointed to happen written in a book in heaven, before even one of them has come to pass (Ps. 139:16). He has taken His time to plan and divinely orchestrated events and days, and this was one of them. After just six months of working making smoothies, I was promoted to manager over the store. I then quit my other job to focus on the growth and management of the store. This did not change my heart for this job; I still disliked it with a strong passion, but I had a bit more purpose now. I knew the Lord was preparing me. I knew that stepping into a position of leadership did not come by accident. Now, I could go on and on about all that the Lord taught and equipped me with in this season of managing an entire store and employees, but I don't want to take away from the main point here, which is the Lord's faithfulness and intentionality. I am still not certain of why I needed to have a season of leadership, but I have some ideas. He was even gracious enough along the way to whisper purpose over situations that crossed my path, giving me strength and courage to endure them.

My desire to shine some light on the topic of submission is that we do not have to understand the reasoning of why we must do something, go somewhere, or, in my case, stay somewhere. We must look up, remember who our God is, and obey. His thoughts are not our thoughts, and His ways are not our ways. (Isa. 55:8) We cannot possibly comprehend the way our God thinks and operates, but He doesn't expect us to either. He just expects us to remember who He is and His past events of faithfulness and know confidently that He never changes.

Application:

I would like us to pray together. I will start, and I want you to finish.

Before we begin, let us assess our hearts. Let's look at our heart posture before we come before the throne of God. We are coming before the King of kings, the Creator of the universe. Let's come and bow in reverence before the God who loves us more than we will ever comprehend.

> *Dear Heavenly Father, please forgive me, Lord, for times and seasons that I was not fully submitted to You, listening for Your instructions. The times that I stepped out before coming to you. Please forgive me for not looking to You first before making a decision. I repent, Father, desiring to turn away from living in my own will and desires and turning only to Your will. Thank you, Lord, for*

having a will for my life. For ordaining, anointing, and divinely working together days for my good and the refining and purifying of my character. Thank you, Father, for Your faithfulness that never changes or wavers, for Your goodness that always pursues and follows me. Thank you, my King, for waiting for me with new mercies every single morning. I praise You Lord forever. You are good, even when I do not understand what or why You are doing something. I know You are good and are greatly to be praised. May praise forever be in my mouth. Lead me today and forever Lord in the way of everlasting. May I walk every day of my life in Your will and for Your glory. I trust You and Your ways. Help me see and believe when I lack faith. I love you, Lord. Thank you for loving me, Lord, even more. In Jesus's name.

Your turn. Close your eyes. Bow down. Cry out from the depth of your heart to your Father who leans down to hear every single word and wipe every single tear. He cares for you.

> Psalm 116:2—"Because He bends down to listen, I will pray as long as I have breath."
>
> 1 Peter 5:7—"Cast all of your anxieties on Him because He cares for you."

DAY 7

Immediate Obedience

Immediate obedience—something I believe is much different than just regular 'ole obedience. It is more significant and can be very telling of our true intentions for the Lord and of our character. I also believe it lets your fellow believers, and God, know if you are indeed dead. Well, for the Lord to be living in You, you must first deny yourself and your flesh. Immediate obedience lets the Lord know if you are a little dead or completely dead. Before you can even think about deciding something or listening to a command, you obey. You do not think about the unction that the Holy Spirit puts on your heart; you just do it. Your flesh is so dead that it does not even have a say or a thought in what to do next; it is the Holy Spirit living in you that begins making decisions. This is a beautiful place for believers to stake out and remain in for as long as they possibly can. I will tell you a cute little story of how immediate obedience played out in my life with the intention and great hope that it will encourage you to dig deeper in surrender to the Lord and seek Him, so He lives more in you. This will enable you to also live out immediate obedience in your daily walk with God.

A couple of weeks ago on the way to work, I came across a homeless woman on the side of the road and felt an impression from the Holy Spirit. He was asking me to do something I had never done before, which was give money to a stranger on the streets. I heard clearly and acted immediately, giving her twenty dollars. Not being in the best financial situation myself, this could have been something I questioned, but I knew I was in a better place than she was, and more than that, I knew what the Lord had said. After driving away, I did not really think much of the situation and was focused on getting in work mode. I went on about the shift waiting tables, and a bit later into the night, I sat with a table of four cops. I had met them a couple of nights before, and we had a good time together, and they decided to come back to see me. We had a great time again, talking about so many things and laughing about even more. When it came time to pay, I grabbed one man's receipt and a few of the other's plates and headed to the back. I dropped the dirty plates in the back, walked to the computer to take care of the ticket I grabbed, looked down at the receipt, and saw $20.00 on the tip line. I almost lost it. I made okay tips at this job, but twenty dollars for one person, this was incredible and such a blessing. I rushed over to the table to meet the four men who had their minds made up already. I could barely get any words out to argue how this was too much before they all blurted out, they had agreed on the amount. They did not care about anything I had to say; they desired to bless me. They all began discussing how much bad they see being cops and because they saw good in me, they wanted to sow into that. They all passed me their receipts with $20.00 written on each tip line. Then it clicked. I had just given a woman on the side of the road twenty dollars being obedient to God, and now I was just given eighty dollars. When I shared what I just realized, one man, not being surprised, responded to me saying, "You see!" Doesn't the Bible say something about giving and then you shall receive blessings?" (I believe he was referring to Luke 6:28.)

It was such an amazing moment for me, filled with so much encouragement and courage to trust God in His commands. This was a small lesson of trusting and obedience, regarding God, that He used to teach me something so crucial. Obey, not only when you want to but whenever He speaks.

This moment led me to wonder how happy we must make Him when we obey, when we give and bless one of His children. How He must smile down upon us in those times. I do not know about you, but I want to do that every single day of my life—make my Father smile. I want to make Him proud in my obedience and my faith. Without faith, it is impossible to please Him, right? (Heb. 11:6)

Application:

I know we have read Psalm 139 before, but our flesh fails us. Psalm 73:26 says, "My flesh and my heart may fail, but God is the strength of my heart and my portion forever." We must seek God with our hearts daily, and sometimes that means reading the same scripture- daily. Watch, something new will arise today. We know we are supposed to become more like Christ, but it is a process. We must continue to be purified and refined so we can look more and more like Him and love more and more like Him.

So, let's search our hearts to see if there are any areas that still have flesh, any wickedness that still lingers trying to alter your thoughts or decisions. To see if any parts of our flesh need to die more so the spirit of God may live more. Read Psalm 139 and pray the last few verses to your Father. Cry out to Him to search you, but then you must surrender to Him so He can remove the wickedness. We must seek Him daily to remove the flesh in us and to ignite the Holy Spirit in us.

> Romans 8:13—"...but if by the Spirit you put to death the deeds of the body, you will live."

_____

_____

_____

Immediate Obedience

DAY 8

A Step of Faith

Some big things have happened all in the past few months, including meeting a new friend named Amber. Amber came into my life a couple months back, and we've been inseparable since. She is a very light-hearted, happy, sweet girl. The very first week of us working together, we were already making plans for her to join me on Sunday for church. The second week, I was working in another store and got a call from my boss saying Amber didn't show up for work and I needed to come in to cover for her. I immediately began to worry because she had just mentioned to me that she was dealing with some serious family issues and even had court that week. I hurried to the other store where my manager was, rehashed my worries, and proceeded to call Amber again. This was so unlike her, to not show up for work and not answer her phone. I felt in my gut that I knew exactly where she was, but I was so afraid to find out if I was right. My manager and I decided to look up county jails near us, and sure enough, Amber and her sweet and scared little face popped up. My heart sank, and I rushed to the back of the store to pray. This sweet girl was in jail, and I did not know why, but I knew it was not right and that I needed to be there for her. Later, her boyfriend called in to say she was sick and would not be coming in. I couldn't help it—I called him to explain my heart for his girlfriend and how I was here to help in any way. We formed a plan together, and a couple hours later and $1,000 dollars in my wallet, we were on our way to jail. We spent hours there waiting and sorting everything out, and finally, I was able to take her home with me. Amber lived with me for a month until she could find her own place. We spent that month growing so close together but also with me pushing her in her faith and being an example of a woman of God to her. I was able to get her a Bible and resources to seek our God herself and, most importantly, I was able to love her so hard, something she knew nothing of. Although she is no longer in my life, I believe the Lord planted so many seeds in her heart in our time together and is still doing much work for her to this day.

I know what you must be thinking. Why would I go out of my way to spend a lot of money to bail out someone I barely knew? Why would I let a stranger into my house? Well, the Lord was leading me and guiding me from the beginning. He was instructing me each step of the way– call her boyfriend back; use my sock money (money I had been saving for the past few months and sticking in a sock). He spoke to me and made a way for her to stay with me. It was a leap of faith to say the least, but I had the comfort and wisdom of the Lord, so I stepped out with confidence. His peace surpasses all understanding, and it doesn't really matter if things don't make sense to others. (Phil. 4:7) If I am being obedient to the Lord and am in His will, then I know I am safe. He has me. No matter what or where it is, if I hear from the Lord, I am doing it. My "yes" is on the table, even before He has spoken to me. My heart is postured toward Him, and my intentions are to please Him and be in His perfect will.

Application:

So, what can we learn from this situation that the Lord clearly had His hand on?

A couple of things, the biggest being boldness for the Lord. Sometimes we must be bold for Him and step out into the (sometimes) uncomfortable place of "faith" to do what He instructs us to. I promise, you will not be let down by the glory that will come when you obey.

How can you tell God "Yes" now before He instructs anything of you?

Why would I want to do this, Summer? Because this is what submitting your life to the Lord looks like, and it is the best place to be! If He is all knowing and the Creator of everything, why would I not want to be exactly where He wants me to be?

In Romans, we read all about us (before we accepted Jesus into our hearts) being slaves to sin at the end of chapter 6. Being enslaved to sin leads to death, but obedience to the Lord leads to righteousness (this just means to be in right standing with God, which can only be done through Jesus Christ). When we give our life to God, we then become slaves to righteousness, obeying His commands and teachings from His heart!

We must live this life day by day, walking by faith and not by sight. We must walk looking through the spiritual eyes given by our Father. This includes visions or dreams He has given you but also a command to step out. We cannot look at things through the lens of this world. If we fall into this trap, it will seem scary and maybe even a little weird to obey some commands He may give you. But if I look at the situation through the faithfulness of my Father's character and the fruit I know will come from this radical obedience and boldness of faith; then I will put my "yes" on the table before He even speaks.

So, can I challenge you? Throw your "yes" out there and watch God move in your life. Write out a simple prayer to God explaining exactly where you are at in this concept of throwing your obedient yes, on the table. Are you ready to throw it out now? Maybe you're not even ready to say yes at all? Talk to Him, tell Him about it. (He would love to hear from you.)

DAY 9

Posture of Waiting

My very first job was a waitressing job. I know I wasn't trained the best, therefore I wasn't the best waitress, but I got the job done. I ensured that each customer who sat at one of my tables was well taken care of to the best of my abilities. My focus during each shift was on my tables. My ear was inclined toward them to hear if they called my name. My eyes were attentive to them for the duration they were there, making sure if they waved me down, I was able to run right over. I brought them their food when it was ready and made sure to refill their drinks when they got low. I conversed with them at times about the mundane things of life. What I learned over time is that one of the goals of waitressing is to bring what the customer needs or wants before he or she voices anything to you. During the hour and a half, they were mine I was going to serve them well, to do just that.

Right now, I am also waiting, but waiting on God, and I am reminded of what it was like to wait on just mere humans. If I have learned anything about seasons of waiting, it's not about what you're waiting on or how long you've been waiting. It's all about *how* you are waiting. God is looking at your heart posture in your waiting season to see how you are waiting—if you are constantly complaining to Him or maybe others around you. Or are you by His side ready for whatever He has you do next? Is your ear postured in a way toward Him in heaven ready to hear whatever He says next? Are your eyes fixed on Him so you will see if He waves you down? Because, my friend, this waiting season is much, much more than just waiting. He is trying to get so much done in you, through you, for you—for you and your future. Wait on Him with a postured heart of patience and perseverance for success in this waiting season.

I remember my first "Waiting Mission" we will call it. I had just moved to Wilmington and was trying my best to find a job. I had applied to so many places before I even moved there and had heard back from only one place. I finally interviewed with them, but of course, it was not just one interview but a total of three. Then I had to wait two more weeks before I heard anything back from them. Talk about waiting on God and learning patience! I had found another job in the meantime: ya know the smoothie one. Anyways, building up to hearing back from the first job and when I could start, I was waiting. For the first part, I was in the *complaining, eye-rolling at God* section of the waiting season. Then, I slowly moved into the "at Your service, God" section. I remember sitting on the couch, pouring out my heart on the matter to my best friend, how it was overwhelming and stressful trying to find a job to pay my bills, but I trusted God and knew He would provide. I was resting in the place of, "I do not care how long I have to wait. I will serve You, and I will wait on You, Lord, because I trust that You are good, and You have a plan." I was sitting back, waiting on God for His move while I was making my moves, which included telling everyone I knew how God was about to show UP in my life. Not a minute later after sending a long text message to my friend about this, I received a call from the first job saying I could go in that week. I had been telling everyone about the faith I had in my God, so I had the chance to go to each person and say, "See, see how faithful our God is?"

    I did wonderful, didn't I? I thought I had conquered being patient. I thought I had passed the tests of trusting God. I really believed that I had been successful in a waiting season, and I was good, until this season. I so effortlessly walked right into another season of waiting, so confused that I began going to my older, wiser friends to explain the situation. I had already learned waiting and patience, but they informed me that this is something our wonderful grace-filled and giving Heavenly Father does regularly. Hmm, isn't that interesting because I did not read that in the handbook!

    Now, the only difference in this season is that I have been in the "at Your service, God" place for a while now, and nothing.

No give or movement. I have been at this place, knowing that He is a good God and a faithful Father who will provide for me and have been resting in the knowledge I have of my God that He will show up when the time is right. Now what?

What do you do when you're waiting and waiting and still waiting? I think of David.

My favorite story in the Bible is the story of David in 1 Samuel. David was a shepherd in his father's pasture. He took care of the sheep and goats daily but always made spending time with the Lord his main priority. So much so that David is known as "The One after God's Own Heart." He was good at stewarding over what God had placed in his hands, and as result, the Lord was able to prepare David for big, big things. Most people know of David from the story of David and Goliath. Well, how do you think he pulled that off? Submission, preparation and, you guessed it, waiting on God and His perfect timing. While David was busy in the field with the sheep and the goats, the Lord was doing much, much more in his life. Bears and lions would come over the hill, and David was able to use what was in his hands to fight them and kill them on multiple occasions. When Goliath was finally presented to David, this was not new for him. It was an effortless act he could perform because David had been prepared and waited on God until He brought the opportunity to him. He grabbed a few stones and slingshot and took Goliath down without a sweat. Perfect example of the significance of stewardship and the purpose of preparation, which is a perfect combination of what it looks like waiting on the timing and plan of God. We must trust the Lord's ways, even if we don't understand and all we see are sheep and goats.

Now, hear me out. My story is nothing like David's, but there are a couple of key moments that happened in his life that I relate to on a serious level. I know that God has big plans for me, and I have a solid idea of what my future is going to be like—speaking to many people about the gospel and our God. Maybe even having a published book or two. Leading people to Christ and discipling people, helping them have a relationship with our Father. Right now, all I see are smoothies. Smoothies. Tell me how smoothies are going to lead to speaking and writing for God exactly? I have finally arrived at a point in my life, though, where I no longer desire to figure it out. I have an easy job of waiting for the promises to come to pass and to just obey when I hear Him call. He knows us—He created us. He knows the exact number of spoilers that we can handle without exploding and ruining everything. It's like that one friend who doesn't know how to keep their mouths shut. You don't plan a surprise birthday party with them, do you? Heck no. You tell them at the last possible moment and give them the smallest amount of information possible so they can show up to the party and not spoil the surprise. This is sometimes why the waiting seasons seem to take much longer than you think.

Application

Proverbs 3:5-6—"Trust in the Lord with all of your heart and lean not on your own understanding."

Habakkuk 2:3—"This vision is for a future time. It describes the end, and it will be fulfilled. If it seems slow in coming, wait patiently, for it will surely take place. It will not be delayed."

Psalm 46:10—"Be still and know that I am God."

Jeremiah 29:11—"'For I know the plans I have for you,' declares the Lord, 'plans to prosper you and not to harm you, plans to give you hope and a future.'"

Isaiah 55:8-9—"'For my thoughts are not your thoughts, neither are your ways my ways,' declares the Lord. 'As the heavens are higher than the earth, so are my ways higher than your ways and my thoughts than your thoughts.'"

Meditate on these scriptures in your season of waiting on the Lord. Maybe you are not in a waiting season right now, but you will be. Prepare yourself for your next one by having these scriptures ingrained in your spirit so you are grounded in the Word of God when you get there. Know who He is. Know that His ways are higher than your ways and His thoughts are higher than your thoughts. He does indeed have a plan, and He does have a purpose for the season that you are in now. Though it may seem to be slow in this season, the vision and the promise will come, and they will not delay. Be still, my friend. Trust Him and His ways, and don't wear yourself out trying to figure it all out.

_____

_____

_____

_____

_____

_____

_____

_____

A Walk With Summer - 15 Day Devotional

DAY 10

Humility

Remember David who we just read and discussed? Something to note about David is that he was very low in humility, and this was a very big deal to the Lord. Picking up where we left off and where we read of David's humility, David was anointed to be king over the nation of Israel but then immediately went back to the pasture. One day, he would eventually become the king, but for right now the Lord was keeping him, teaching him, and preparing him. For David, this was a test that most of us would have failed, to say the least. He had been anointed to be king of Israel but was now expected to almost go backwards and still work for his father in the pasture. Later, he even got an opportunity to go to the palace, the place where his purpose was waiting for him, but not to be king, to serve. If we rewind to before David was anointed as king, Samuel, who was a prophet at the time, had just gotten word from God that His anointing was being lifted off Saul and Samuel needed to go to Jesse's house to anoint the new king. Jesse got all his sons together to present to Samuel… but David. God said no to all of Jesse's sons, so Samuel had to specifically ask if there were any other sons. Jesse responded yes but that he was just the youngest and was in the pasture. You see how David was valued by even his father and brothers? This was the theme of David's life, but the following verse became the new theme of it. David was sent for, then he was anointed. This caused humility to automatically be a characteristic of David's life, but that was not enough for God and for where David was going. Anointing of elevation requires humility to be sown into every facet of your heart. So, how did God do this in David? He anointed him then sent him back.

The Lord has anointed me and for much more than I am seeing right now. He anointed me in showing me visions of my future. Then what? He sent me to smoothies; one could possibly say that's very similar to sheep and goats…and I could very much agree. This story of David is something I have hung on to and that has kept me moving through the smoothies, pushing through the humility being so aggressively woven into every crevice of my character. I had this hope that the Lord was doing it for a reason and the strength to let the process of the promise unfold slowly day by day, smoothie by smoothie.

We know that pride is the opposite of being humble. Pride puts significance and importance on one's achievements or self. The credit for the achievements we have in life should only go to one place and that is to the God who created us. When we have pride, we are snatching credit from God and putting it on ourselves as if we are the reason it happened. Pride also blocks communication with the Lord. I truly believe that pride disgusts the Lord. If pride is something that is a part of your character and, worse, your heart, seek the Lord now. Proverbs 11:2 says that pride was in fact the very first sin, and I believe it stuck with God and is something that causes Him great hurt.

Now, no shame in acknowledging this but conviction yes. Conviction of God is such a blessing we must lean into. His conviction comes out of love and pierces our heart with grace. We must acknowledge that pride is a sin, it does not please God and it puts a barrier between us. We must repent and lay it before the Lord, and He will help us.

Application:

Humility is a low view of one's own importance. Biblical humility is having a low importance level on who you are AND leaning on who you are in God.

Is humility something you could classify yourself as having? Or being humble?

What are some ways you can incorporate humility in your heart and actions daily?

Ask Him to reveal the areas of your heart and life that contain pride. Bring them to the surface of your heart and to the feet of Jesus. May we rebuke the pride in our lives daily and ask God to intervene and bring humility to those areas, giving Him opportunity to move freely in them.

> 1 Peter 5:6—"Humble yourselves, therefore, under God's mighty hand, that he may lift you up in due time."

> Colossians 3:1—"Since, then, you have been raised with Christ, set your hearts on things above, where Christ is, seated at the right hand of God."

> Proverbs 3:34—"He mocks proud mockers but shows favor to the humble and oppressed."

> James 4:10—"Humble yourself before the Lord, and He will lift you up."

Memorize and meditate on these. Write out what God reveal to you while you do it.

_____

_____

_____

_____

Humility

A Walk With Summer - 15 Day Devotional

DAY 11

Pregnant with a Promise

I am not sure if I have made it clear enough, but I do not like or enjoy my job at all! The biggest reason that I do not like it is because I feel like it pushes me away from God when my biggest goal in life is that I would grow closer to Him every single day. So, this really bugs me, on top of all the other pieces of my job that make it miserable. This job is so pressing on every side that I literally step out of my Christian self into someone who does not control her actions or words. I am not myself when I am there, and I know I am not who God wants me to be when I am there. I just get so angry and stressed that I have no control over what I do. I just hate this job, I really do. But – it is the exact place that God wants me in this season of my life, and it is the place of preparation for the promises to come to pass that He has placed in me. What is there to hate about that? I want to love it, and I know the Lord wants me to along with bringing light to a dark place. To make a difference there.

When I take my eyes out of world mode and into heavenly perspective, I see that it is the place of preparation and a sifting season for my heart. He tends to use heat to enable these impurities in your heart to rise to the surface. I can with confidence say that there is heat applied to me at my job. I can also see, with these heavenly goggles the Lord lets me borrow sometimes, that He has divinely placed specific young people there for me to love, encourage, and build up to the best of my ability. What a blessing in disguise it is. A disguise? Yes, these children are crazy! So, anyways, I really do try my best to keep these goggles on, but wow, it is like every time I place them on my face securely and look up, the fire around me burns them up, and all I can see is fire again. Staring at fire most of your day can be very frustrating and can make one very stressed and act out of character. But we cannot. This is a test, my friend, I do know that for sure. He is looking to see what exactly I will do, with the work that He has placed in my hands at this time. Have the nerve to do a pretty good job? Then He decides to crank the heat up and see how you steward over the work when a little pressure is applied. All of this has been made very clear to me, but that does not mean I am walking through this with flying colors. It is still a battle every single day, but I trust the Lord and the process to the promise, so I lean in and keep going.

 The other day, I watched this sermon on waiting, and the pastor made a parallel that was very encouraging to me at this time. He compared a woman going through labor and birthing her child to a miracle God places in us. He compared the two because the miracles and promises God places in us sometimes can seem to go through the same process of being birthed. There is a process necessary for the baby, or the promise, to grow before it comes out into the world. There is preparation that is necessary for the mom of the unborn baby and for you who are pregnant with the promise. When a woman is pregnant, for the first few months, she can get away with nobody knowing that there is something, someone growing inside of her. As time goes on and the baby continues to grow in her, however, there comes a moment when she can no longer get away with this. Everyone around her knows that she is pregnant, wondering just when she is going to "pop." There is a knowing, by everyone around her, that one day, this baby growing in her will indeed come out. One way or another, we all know that when the time is right, that baby will come out of the woman and into the world.

Now, in this time of pregnancy, the woman and her husband are preparing for the baby. They will begin "nesting." Nesting occurs in pregnant women as they have strong urges to prepare for the baby that is coming soon. It is even said that as the urges grow stronger and stronger to prepare for the baby, that labor is soon to follow.

When labor does finally come, the woman begins having contractions, preparing to now push the baby out. She is in immense amounts of pain as her body is doing exactly what it needs to do to release the baby into the world. As she gets closer and closer to being fully prepared to have the baby, the pain increases. She will begin bearing down, positioning herself to finally release the baby. She pushes and pushes the baby slowly out of her, down the dark birth canal until the baby's head is visible. Again, there is no question of the doctors wondering, "Oh no, maybe the baby won't come out." One way or another, the baby must come out of the woman. Maybe the baby will come out in a different way than they were expecting, in a different timeline than they thought, but the arguable fact is, the baby will come out. The woman finally finishes pushing and gives birth to her baby.

Our spiritual lives can very much be a parallel of this beautiful concept of life. There are promises, visions, and dreams that have been placed in you by the Lord, and they will come out. Now, I can only speak of my own life and what the Lord has done and is doing, but I can relate to this concept here. I do believe that when I said "yes" to God, He placed a promise in me. These seasons of life I am going through now are like the early months of a woman's pregnancy. Nobody around me knows I am pregnant with a promise, and honestly, sometimes I even question if there is something in me growing. But my God cannot lie, so I put my faith in not the unseen forming of the promise in me, but on the Word of God. As the months go on in my life, I can see that some of those around me have eyes to see my small little belly being the promise or anointing placed in me. As this promise in me is slowly being grown and formed by the hands of God, I am "nesting" for this promise to come to pass. I am getting myself and my life ready so when the promise is birthed into the world, I am ready for it. I can feel the pressure growing and growing to nest more and more as the tests are passed and my character is being molded. I know one day, before I know it, it will be time for me to start pushing. I want to make sure I am ready to hold, neuter, and take care of this promise that will be entrusted to me, to make sure my hands and character are strong enough to steward over it well. I want to make sure its home, being the temple that is me, is ready to inhabit this promise. Do you see now?

Why it is getting painful for me, the contractions being applied to this season as I am bearing down to go to the next contraction or season of life. I am getting ready. I am getting prepared.

Are you?

Application:

Sometimes the things of life can be distracting and take our focus off the promises the Lord once clearly told us and put our focus on the hardships of life. Sometimes it can be so distracting at times that we can forget the visions He has shown us or the dreams He has given us. We completely forget where we are going and why, or we doubt the promises stated throughout His Word.

Let us take some time today to write down and meditate on the promises the Lord has given us.

Habakkuk 2:2 says to write the revelation (vision) down and make it plain on tablets so that whoever may run with it. Let us write every single vision down, every single dream birthed in our spirits. Write down all the promises of God. Now!! Say them out loud and come to an agreement with them. Watch this change your perspective and watch yourself pick up these heavenly goggles and rock your world and the season you are living in right now for God.

Get ready for the baby. Start bearing down and preparing for it to come because though it may linger, WAIT because it will come and not delay. It will come (Hab. 2:3).

Begin to memorize and meditate on these scriptures for today.

Can I challenge you? Read these out loud daily for the next week. Let's watch how your perspective so quickly shifts and your heart posture changes!

_____

_____

_____

_____

_____

DAY 12
Depressed and Distant

The last time I wrote was when another hurricane was about to hit us. It has been a while because I have found myself slipping back into another depression. This one is rough. I have not been this depressed since giving my life to God. *Summer, do you mean you can still struggle with depression as a Christian?* Oh yeah. Maybe even worse than a non-believer, as we do gain a target on our back by the enemy to be distracted from the things of God. I am in a place where I can feel myself coming out of it and hope getting closer, but then back I will go into hopelessness and lots of darkness. The hope is not yet near enough to grab hold of, but it seems so easy for me to grab hold of dark thoughts and sadness.

So, what do you do when you are depressed and distance yourself from those around you? What do you do when you do not want to reach out and ask for help or prayer? When all you want to do is stay in your room alone and sink deeper into the pain? That is exactly what I did and for the longest time. I couldn't ask for prayer for the depression I was in like the Christian who I claimed to be. No way! People would judge me and look down on me and question my salvation, like I already was. But, I knew what I needed to do, so I reached out. Just sharing it, I could feel myself starting to come out. The community that was there on the other side of me sharing the darkness of my present, met me with love and encouragement. They were there to love me, build me up, and be there for me, and slowly, I could feel myself getting better. Hope was still very vague, and my mental and spiritual health were still hanging on by a thread. I can feel myself still on the edge of breaking. I know that I took my eyes off the Lord and put them on my situations and what my circumstances looked like. They looked rough so, of course, I slipped into sadness.

That is how I got here; in case you were wondering. Already having weak mental health, if I just for a second look away from God and look to the tragic circumstances of my life, I oh so effortlessly jump into a hole of darkness. I am still going to church and putting a smile on my face, acting as though everything is grand. I am still in the Word and watching sermons but with no hope in sight. It has been such a long season of God being silent in my life. Before, I could not hear Him, but I could very much see Him and His hand working in my life. Well, now, it's like I can barely see Him at all. He is distant, and I am depressed but faithful. This means no matter how low the hope meter gets; I will be a faithful follower of

Christ and trust that He still has ahold of me. But at times I have found myself telling God that this is not what I signed up for, asking Him why I must struggle so much. Isn't that just depressing in itself? Well, Summer, I hate to break it to you, but you did sign up for this. More specifically, you signed up for suffering. When you said yes to God, you said yes to His will for your life. And those visions, dreams, and promises He has given you—if you want those to come to pass, you must pass through these troubled waters. This is for the kingdom of God and all the people you will one day impact and empower in their own walk with God. So, I keep going. I press on and with my eyes up and focused on things above.

Application:

Depression; being hopeless. Losing your hope for the future.

We must remind ourselves daily of what the Word says to protect ourselves from this dangerous place that will keep us from walking in the fullness of being a daughter of the King.

Let's pray.

> *Heavenly Father, praise You, my King. Thank you, Father, for all that You are. Perfection, Lord, is what You are. Praise you, Lord, for walking with me with Your hand in mine. Please switch my*

perspective and secure it in Your goodness. May my heart posture be toward heaven and pleasing You. May I be kneeling before Your throne so that I may remember what I am doing on earth. Lord, turn my chin up to the heavens, and may I never look back down at my circumstance. May You give me new revelations of the assignments and tasks You have for me on earth so that I may not lose focus and may not waver in my walk and where I am headed. Lord, realign me so that I may line up with You and You, alone.

I ask all of this in Your Son Jesus's name, Amen.

DAY 13

Darkness of the Roots

I hate to admit it, but here I am again in a place where I am struggling. I have really seemed to find myself in another pit. I also must admit exactly how I got here; I have been listening to the enemy. I have. I have been listening to his lies, forgetting the truth of the Lord. I have been singlehandedly giving my mind over to the enemy himself, letting him play recess on the playground that has become my mind. Embarrassing to write, but it is true. I want to make it clear exactly how I got here because I could assume that is exactly how you stepped into the pit you may be in right now, too.

Can I remind you of something? That even though it may be your fault that you are in this place, can I remind you of where your God is as well? Right beside you. Yes, you read that right. He jumped right into that pit with His daughter, and He isn't going anywhere. Now, you want to get out. Simple. Stop looking at the pit that you are in, in the miry depths of the hole you are dwelling in with thoughts of darkness and turn around and look to God. Look at Him and say, "I surrender." Allow Him into the situation so He may intervene. He is not going to intervene in a life and situation He is not welcomed in.

I know it is tough. It is discouraging right now in a season of sifting that seems to be a season of stagnation. Believe me, I understand, but do you know what I have come to understand even more? The Lord's faithfulness. He is faithful even when things seem to be still, and He seems silent. He is faithful, and He is your Father. The game-changing shift in this season you are dwelling in occurs when you focus on this knowledge and *fix* your focus on the face of your Father. Stop looking around at the storms of your life and at everything not going right. Maybe things seem not to be going right because they are not fitting your expectations for how this season ought to go or what you desired. That is risky business and will get you in a season of doubt, I can write with confidence and from experience. The Lord's ways and thoughts are above ours. Isaiah 55 describes how the Lord's thoughts and ways are not our ways. He works in ways that we could never understand, and if we try to, we get ourselves into a whirlwind of confusion and frustration. "Be still and know that I am God" (Ps. 46:11). Do you know how to live this out? Be quiet. Know that you *know* that you *know* that the God of the universe is your God, and He has you. Sit down and be quiet and keep doing what He told you to do last that you haven't even been working on because you were too busy complaining to Him. Watch your life change. Watch yourself get back all the energy you have lost over this past season.

Seeing no progress but hearing that progress is happening—that is what we must focus on when God changes frames. He steps out of the frame you are used to seeing Him in, to a different frame to communicate in a different way. When He steps out and now you see nothing, you must lean into what you are hearing. Be still, be super quiet, and wait to hear Him speak.

When I think about how I lack to see change from day to day, I think about children growing up. Stare at a child every day, and you also will not see much change. Go one month, or better yet, one year, and the changes that you will see are great. Physically, there are changes in their voice and how they talk. Emotionally, there is stability being built in them. What about watching a tree grow after you plant a seed in the ground? Depending on the climate of the tree, it could take thirty years for a tree to be fully grown. When a seed is planted in the ground, it could take six weeks for anything to even sprout out of the ground. Six weeks for deep, strong roots to be woven into the earth and another thirty years for it to be fully grown. And that is just for trees in warm climates; trees that are planted in cooler climates can take hundreds of years to reach full growth. I asked myself, why would trees in colder climates require more time for growth? Cooler climates cause colder conditions. If those trees do not have thick, strong roots and a nice, sturdy trunk with every single limb being strong and limber, they will not last a day. The climate and atmosphere that they are entering into requires more steadiness. More strength, deeper roots.

The roots that are required for what the Lord has for you require a strength that comes from God. What are the ways the Lord instills this strength in you? You guessed it! Storms. But with the required roots, it does not matter what storms come after; these roots can withstand anything. Rain, tornadoes, hurricanes, cold, dry seasons—these trees withstand. So, they go through growth and preparation for it. It may seem as though there is no change or fruits visible to the outside, but maybe the Lord is forming your roots underneath the surface, in your heart. Maybe there is much fruit coming from your life but on the inside of you. Your heart and character are being worked on right now, and you cannot see because you are not looking there.

Application:

Remember who you were before you knew the Lord, how you were lost and, in the world, searching to fill the void that can only be filled by God. Do you remember what you were like? How were you treating people? The lack of fruit your character had and your heart that was wicked and deceitful.

Now, who are you today? Look at your heart now and the way you love people. There is much fruit that has been reaped every day you've run to the Lord. For us to love people better, we must understand the love of God and know how to receive His love. All of this is done by spending time in the presence of God. This is what causes fruit to start bearing on the roots growing in the grounds of our heart. It also causes God to do some sifting to the fruit that is dead. We must start at the roots. Lean into these beautiful changes being done under the surface.

> 2 Corinthians 4:17—"For our light and momentary troubles are achieving for us an eternal glory that far outweighs them all."

> 1 Peter 5:10—"And the God of all grace, who called you to his eternal glory in Christ, after you have suffered a little while, will himself restore you and make you strong, firm and steadfast."

_____

_____

_____

_____

A Walk With Summer - 15 Day Devotional

DAY 14

A Test of Your Heart

It has been a long time since I last wrote, but it has been a very long, dry desert season. I am wondering about this one. I went through a season of deep depression, and I finally made it out and walked myself into a season of numbness. I felt nothing. No anger or frustration, but also no peace or joy. Nothing from Lord or Him being near me even. In a community group the other day, I was explaining to them this season I have been in, how I have walked the past couple years with God and Him right by my side. Almost on the couch right beside me just chatting the whole way. Now, the shift that has happened is like Jesus is on the couch but the one across the room with His arms crossed looking over to me, waiting to see what exactly I will do as He draws away. He has not left me, and He is very much keeping a close eye on me and saying a few words if needed, but even those are difficult to hear and seem to be coming from afar. I no longer hear Him clearly, and

I also no longer have the comfort of His presence. Jesus sitting on the couch across the way with His arms folded, I can almost clearly hear Him saying, "Okay, Summer, now what? What are you going to do now with the tools I have given you?" Like what God did to King Hezekiah "to see what was in his heart" (2 Chron. 32:31).

Application:

What will you do when the Lord decides to pull His presence away from you? Will you get frustrated and start to complain? Or back away from Him because you no longer have the comfort of His presence?

A devoted heart to the Lord will not run away in frustration but run toward Him out of faithfulness, which is what He desires. He has not drawn away from you; He has just taken your ability to feel Him , to see exactly what is in your heart.

How can you lean into Him to show Him you trust His process of testing, showing Him the trueness of your heart toward Him, which is loving Him no matter what?

John 6:26 shows us that the Lord does know our hearts and their intentions, so faking it will not work here. He really desires to reveal the truth of our hearts for Him and our intentions. Are we devoted to the Lord for the promise He gave or because we received His love and desire to live for Him? Genesis 22 shows how God tested just that with Isaac to Abraham.

Read Genesis 22 and write down what the Holy Spirit highlights to you in the story.

How can these things also be applied to your life, trial, or heart?

_____

_____

_____

_____

_____

_____

_____

_____

_____

_____

_____

A Walk With Summer - 15 Day Devotional

DAY 15

Wait & Praise

A quick recap to what the previous week entailed for me. It included rushing from work to baby sit for a couple from church but running behind. I was almost running late when my phone with GPS decided to freeze, and I had no idea where to go. I was upset in the moment and reacted. I chucked my phone across my car, okay, I did it. Well not a good idea because it completely broke my phone. Now what, right? I couldn't do anything besides try my best to drive back home. I am not even kidding on the way back with tear filled eyes and the windows down I hear a weird sound. It was my tire, and it was going down. I literally got a flat tire. I pull over to double check it is flat and form together some plan. I am trying my best to mess with my phone to see if I can call someone and it worked. You know who my phone called? The cops, it called 9-1-1. I couldn't turn it off, so I had to try to choke back my tears to explain to the operator that I was fine. Finally, we get off the phone, but it doesn't stop there people. My phone sends SOS messages to all my emergency contacts. My sister. My mom. My stepmom. Somehow my phone was able to call my sister who was freaking out and was able to calm her own and let her know that I was okay. Long story short she was able to get ahold a couple of my friends in town and they came to the rescue. We got the tire changed. I got my phone fixed the next day. All was well.

There are things to be thankful for in a situation like this, and that is something I had to hang on to. I have a phone and a car that can be broken or damaged. I have a job with an income that will allow me to pay to repair these things. Most of all, I am so thankful for a God who loves me so much that He would not only allow these things to grow me, but He would work it all together for my good. He loves me enough to allow me to go through temporary frustration and hurt for the eternal glory that is becoming more like His Son, Jesus. I am so thankful for His love and His hand in my life, even when it is in difficult ways.

The place that I am in now after this past week, I do not want to say is frustration or confusion, but I am not content or comfortable. I am not comfortable right now. I just constantly replay James 1 and Jeremiah 29:11 on repeat in my heart, and I do believe that is why I even made it to Monday. Just to be clear though, I am not okay. I am not in a place that I desire to be with God right now. I am trying so hard to be sensitive to the Holy Spirit, and all I am hearing is, "Wait on Me." All I can say back is "wait on You for what, God? For what?"

On top of all that *was* last week, I basically got kicked out of the house I was staying at. At a house who held a couple who have loved me so well and taken care of me. A place that I was shocked to have stay so long but they decided it was time for me to leave. They believed I was getting comfortable and not working towards the move to Texas that God made clear to me. They were trying their best to love me well and this is what it looked like to them. It is not that I am not working towards the move, this is what waiting on God looks like. It doesn't seem to be very popular to us humans. Waiting on God can look stagnant and ineffective. I can assure you- it is so effective, and it is one of the best places we can be, waiting on God. I am trusting God and His God's timing not interested in making things happen myself, and some people could not see it clear enough.

Maybe this wasn't the worst week in history, but it was a fire applied to my season—a season that my life feels up in the air in every single area of my life. A season lacking stability and consistency, and the Lord turns up the heat to see what happens. He tends to turn up the heat when nearing the end of a season approaching a new level. He will apply this said "heat" to see exactly what you do and what impurities rise to the surface.

What can we do when heat is applied to an already frustrating and sensitive season? Well, the only thing we can do- praise and worship the King. Why? Because of all that He has done in your life and all that is documented in the Word. David wrote in Psalm 52 verse 9, "I will praise you for what you have done in the past, always." This should also be the posture of our hearts, especially in the seasons that seem to be hard pressing on every side. When all things seem to be caving in and crumbling to dust, praise Him. He deserves our praise no matter where we are and what circumstances we are in, always.

Application:

Are you in a sifting season like this now?

Write a letter to God of all that you are thankful for that He has done in your past. The faithfulness that You have seen time and time again. The faithfulness you have read throughout the Bible time and time again. Because their testimony is also your testimony—you serve the same God!

_____

_____

_____

_____

_____

_____

_____

_____

_____

_____

Ask Him then to reveal the impurities that He is gracefully, with love, trying to remove. Thank Him for loving you enough to spend time to remove these impurities and bless your life, spending time planning and leading your life every single day.

> Jeremiah 1:5— "Before I formed you in the womb I knew you, before you were born, I set you apart; I appointed you as a prophet to the nations."

> Psalm 139:16—"Your eyes saw my unformed body; all the days ordained for me were written in your book before one of them came to be."

Cry out to Him to shift your heart posture to see the goodness He is pouring out in your life during the fire. Anything else that is on your heart, tell Him. He is listening.

And of course, praise Him. Praise Him because He is good. Always and forever, especially in the midnight hour.

DAY 16

Final Recap

Well, my friend, we have reached the end. The end of our fifteen-day endeavor to get closer to the heart of God and go deeper into our kneel of surrender before His throne. Wow, I can't believe it!

How are you? How has your heart shifted in the throne room of heaven? Please take some time to reflect on who you were before beginning this journey and how the Lord has gracefully impacted you. How have you healed? Your perspective shifted?

_____

_____

_____

_____

Goodbye

Woman of God, I could weep thinking of the possible impact that my words could have made on your life. I could sit and cry with the passion that I must do just that in your life. You, who are reading this, are special to me, believe it or not. You, daughter of God, is why I was sent to this world and to these specific years of the world spinning. For you and for such a time as this- *you* would be reading a collection of chapters called my life so you could ever so slightly be encouraged. Be empowered. Be impacted and hopefully receive more of the Lord's love.

I hope you are burning now. On fire for God but woman of God, don't stop here. Don't stop burning right here. Keep going! We are on a mission to change the world, and it begins with impacting the people in our life right now! Love them today and love them hard. Forgive them now. Spend time with Jesus. Run after Him and the things He reveals to you. Keep looking up to Him and don't stop because you, well; you are changing the world,

I am just sent here to open your eyes to see it.

Connecting With Summer

If this book has made any impact on your life, please let me know. I would love for you to share how the Lord turned hard times in my life for good by impacting you in any way. I'd endure it all over again if it meant your life would be changed in some way!

You can email me here or find me on Instagram and message me!

summer.d.wilks@gmail.com

Please remember, you are more valuable than precious diamonds that flood the earth with their beauty and rarity. You, woman of God, are anointed to bring hope. You have an anointing so powerful to shake up the earth. Let Him lead you, and watch it happen.

Xo Summer

CPSIA information can be obtained
at www.ICGtesting.com
Printed in the USA
LVHW100010300722
724731LV00001B/2